**is for the Arctic Fox.**

They live in northern Canada.

Arctic foxes fur coat is white in the winter, but in the summer it is brown.

They can hear prey under the snow, they'll jump high and dig through the snow to find it.

is for the North American Beaver

They live in Canada south of the tree line.

The North American Beaver is the national animal of Canada.

Beaver have orange teeth that do not stop growing; they use them to cut down trees.

My First Book about the Animal Alphabet of Canada

Amazing Animal Books Children's Picture Books

By Molly Davidson

Mendon Cottage Books

JD-Biz Publishing

Read More Amazing Animal Books

Purchase at Amazon.com

Download Free Books!
http://MendonCottageBooks.com

C is for Caribou.

Caribou live in the Boreal forests that stretch across Canada.

Caribou are also called reindeer; and both the boys and the girls have antlers.

They can run 50 mph, when escaping predators.

D is for a Common Dolphin.

They can be found in the North Atlantic Ocean.

White-beaked common dolphins like to eat squid and school of fish.

They have a white belly to camouflage with the bright sun as predators are looking up at the surface of the ocean.

E is for an Elk (Wapiti).

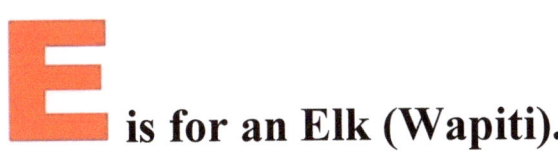

They live in the southern Rockies and prairies.

Bull (boy) elk stand about 4 1/2 feet tall, to their shoulders, they weigh up to 750 pounds, and their antlers can be up to 4 1/2 feet long.

F is for a Fur Seal.

They live along the rocky shores of British Columbia.

Boys can weigh up to 600 pounds; the girls weigh only about 120 pounds.

When they are at sea, they sleep on their backs.

 **G** is for the Canadian Goose.

The Canadian goose spends the summers in the southern Canadian provinces.

They live about 24 years in the wild.

When they migrate they fly in a "V" formation.

H

is for a Short-tailed Weasel, also called a Hermine.

They can be found in most of Canada, except the southern prairies and Anticosti Island.

The short-tailed weasel eats voles, hamsters, pikas, and sometimes birds, insects, and lizards.

I is for a Thirteen - Lined Ground Squirrel which has the scientific name of Ictidomys Tridecemlineatus.

It lives in the southern provinces on the prairies.

They live in burrows with only a 2 inch opening.

J  is for a White-tailed Jackrabbit.

White-tailed jackrabbits live in the southern prairies and in Okanagan Valley.

They can run up to 40 mph and jump 10 feet with one leap.

 **is for a bat called the Keen's Myotis.**

USNPS © <u>Wikimedia Commons</u>

They live on the west coast of British Columbia.

They get their name from Reverend Keen who did research in finding this species.

L is for a Canadian Lynx.

The Canadian Lynx lives in most parts of Canada.

They can see prey up to 250 feet away

Lynx hunt alone and usually at night.

 **is for a Moose.**

They live in the areas from the Yukon to New Brunswick.

Moose eat up to 73 pounds of plants per day.

Their antlers can weigh up to 40 pounds.

 is for a Narwhal.

Glenn Williams © <u>Wikimedia Commons</u>

They live in the oceans north of Quebec and Nunavut.

Narwhals usually live with 20 - 30 others, but when migrating it might be up to 1,000 narwhals.

O is for the Northern River Otter.

Otters live in most of the rivers and lakes in Canada, except in the Arctic.

They can dive up to 60 feet underwater.

Their pelts are waterproof, which helps keep them warm.

P is for a Pronghorn.

They live in southern Saskatchewan and Alberta.

Pronghorn are the fastest mammals in North America; they can run up to 60 mph.

Boys and girls both have forked antlers.

 **is for a Quail.**

Species of quail live in the southern part of British Columbia and southern Ontario.

Quails lay 10 - 20 eggs at a time.

They can only fly short distances.

R is for a Red Squirrel.

They live south of the tree line, in British Columbia, Vancouver, and Cape Breton Islands.

Red squirrels shed their heavy winter coats every spring, and grow it back in the fall.

S is for a Silver-Haired Bat.

LassenNPS © <u>Wikimedia Commons</u>

They live throughout of the southern Canada.

About 20% of all mammals in Canada are a type of bat!

They weigh the same as two nickels (8-12 g).

T

is for a Badger, whose scientific name is Taxidea Taxus.

Badgers live on the prairies of Ontario and British Columbia.

They are mean animals and can resist snake venom.

U is for a Ungava Collard Lemming.

Argus Fin © <u>Wikimedia Commons</u>

These lemmings live in northern Quebec.

Mother lemmings have 2 or 3 sets of 4 - 8 babies per year.

U

is for an Brown Bear who has the scientific name of Ursus Arctos. (*Bonus U)

The brown bear lives in Nunavut and the Rockies.

They are the largest bears weighing up to 1,400 pounds.

 **is for a Vole.**

They live in Quebec, British Columbia, Ontario, and the Yukon.

Voles live in colonies of up to 300!

Most voles die within a week of birth and the others only live for 3 to 6 months.

 is for a Gray Wolf.

The gray wolf lives all over Canada, but is quickly becoming extinct in many areas.

Wolf packs will travel up to 12 1/2 miles per day hunting prey.

The wolf is the largest member of the dog family.

X is the last letter in Musk oX.

Musk oxen live in the Canadian arctic.

Their hooves are so strong they can break through solid ice.

They are related to sheep and goats.

 **is for a Yellow - Bellied Marmot.**

Yellow-bellied marmots live in British Columbia and Alberta.

They are about the size of a house cat, weighing 11 pounds.

Marmots hibernate in burrows during the winter.

Z is for Cuvier's Beaked Whale whose scientific name is Ziphius Carvirostris.

NMFS Southwest Fisheries Science Center © Wikimedia Commons

They swim in the northern Pacific and Atlantic Oceans.

The boys have two large teeth they use to fight for the girls.

Download Free Books!

http://MendonCottageBooks.com

Purchase at Amazon.com
Website http://AmazingAnimalBooks.com

Horses For Kids
Amazing Animal Books For Young Readers
By John and Annalee Davidson

Ponies For Kids
Amazing Animal Books
Rachel Smith

Ten Amazing Horses For Kids
Nature Books for Kids
JD-Biz Publishing
K. Bennett

Akhal-Teke "The Golden Horse of the desert" For Kids
Nature Books for Kids
JD-Biz Publishing
K. Bennett

Suffolk-Punch "The Gentle Giant" For Kids
Nature Books for Kids
JD-Biz Publishing
K. Bennett

Shires "The great Horse" For Kids
Nature Books for Kids
JD-Biz Publishing
K. Bennett

Colonial Spanish "Horse of the Americas" For Kids
Nature Books for Kids
JD-Biz Publishing
K. Bennett

Canadian "The Little Iron Horse" For Kids
Nature Books for Kids
JD-Biz Publishing
K. Bennett

Cleveland Bays "History and Future" Horses For Kids
Nature Books for Kids
JD-Biz Publishing
K. Bennett

Our books are available at

1. Amazon.com

2. Barnes and Noble

3. Itunes

4. Kobo

5. Smashwords

6. Google Play Books

Download Free Books!
http://MendonCottageBooks.com

Publisher

JD-Biz Corp

P O Box 374

Mendon, Utah 84325

http://www.jd-biz.com/